AF260933

Foreword

Why Two Minute Questions?

When I was a kid, I used to order these Scholastic mysteries from the school. They were these little, thin paperbacks, like 50-60 or so pages, much like what you're holding now, that had a short mystery written on a page. Usually they consisted of some story and then a question. How did someone get killed? Where did the murder weapon go? Something like that. You then turned the page to find out the answer after thinking about it for a minute.

We now bring you Volume 5 of our SQL Server Stumpers and, once again, that's what we're trying to build here, but instead of some mystery, it's a quiz type format of SQL Server questions and answers, culled from the annals of our very popular Question of the Day on the SQLServerCentral.com website. These are a collection of questions from the past that we put together to help you study for an exam, learn a bit more about SQL Server, pass the time, etc. But they're mostly collected for…

The INTERVIEW.

You're looking for a new job; you've posted your resume, worked on cover letters, and finally landed an interview. Now you want to be sure that you look your best; that you can answer what's thrown at you.

I can't promise that anyone will ask you any of these questions, but you never know. Maybe some managers that are interviewing will grab a copy of the book and start asking questions out of it. But it will help you prepare, give you some hands on experience, challenge you in a variety of ways about the different aspects of SQL Server. Some of the questions are arcane, some very common, but you'll learn something and the wide range of questions will help you get your mind agile and ready for some quick thinking.

This version is a compilation of SQL Server 2005 and SQL Server 2008 questions, to bring you up to date on the latest version of SQL Server.

So read on, in order, randomly, just start going through them, but do yourself a favor and think about each before turning the page. Challenge yourself and see how well you do.

Thanks for your support and be sure to visit us online.

Steve Jones

SQLServerCentral.com

Question 1

You want to implement a fast parse of some data in SQL Server 2005 Integration Services, but are concerned it is not supported. Which of the following formats are not supported?

Choose one of the answers below:

1. Leading plus signs, like "+7".

2. Leading minus signs, like "-12".

3. Trailing spaces, like "10".

4. Hexadecimal numbers, like "4A".

Answer:

4. Hexadecimal numbers, like "4A".

Explanation:

A fast parse does not allow special characters like $, nor does it support scientific notation, hexadecimal formats, or white space characters like leading spaces.

Ref: Numeric Data Formats - **http://msdn2.microsoft.com/en-us/library/ms141729.aspx**

Question 2

In SQL Server 2005 Integration Services, what happens to the checkpoint file each time the package is executed from the beginning?

Choose one of the answers below:

1. A new checkpoint file is created.

2. If a file exists, data is appended to it, otherwise a new one is created.

3. A new file is created and the old one is renamed to [packagename].1, like log files.

Answer:

1. A new checkpoint file is created.

Explanation:

The checkpoint file is recreated anew on each package execution.

Ref: Using Checkpoints in Packages -
http://msdn2.microsoft.com/en-us/library/ms 140226.aspx

Question 3

What does @@total_write in SQL Server 2005?

Choose one of the answers below:

1. The total number of writes (disk + cached) for the previous statement.

2. The total number of writes (disk only) for the previous statement.

3. The total number of writes (disk + cached) for the instance since last restart.

4. The total number of writes (disk only) for the instance since last restart.

Answer:

4. The total number of writes (disk only) for the instance since last restart.

Explanation:

The @@total_read function returns the number of disk writes since the SQL Server instance was last restarted.

Ref: @@total_read -
http://msdn2.microsoft.com/en-us/library/ms 187917.aspx

Question 4

When you implement a group of Federated Database Servers in SQL Server 2005, how are you gaining scale?

Choose one of the answers below:

1. Scale-Up

2. Scale-Out

3. Scale-Around

4. Scale-Beyond

Answer:

2. Scale-Out

Explanation:

A group of Federated Database Servers works by scaling out your servers.

Ref: Understanding Federated Database Servers - **http://msdn2.microsoft.com/en-us/library/ms 187467.aspx**

Question 5

How many network cards do you need per cluster node in a server cluster?

Choose one of the answers below:

1. One

2. Two

3. Three

4. Four

Answer:

2. Two

Explanation:

A server cluster requires at least two physically separate network cards.

Ref: Page 121 of **Pro SQL Server 2005 High Availability**
Windows Server 2003 Clustering -
**http://www.microsoft.com/windowsserver2003/te
chinfo/overview/bdmtdm/default.mspx**

Question 6

Which is the first version of SQL Server to incorporate log shipping as a feature?

Choose one of the answers below:

1. 4.21a

2. 6.5

3. 7

4. 2000

Answer:

4. 2000

Explanation:

This was the first version in which log shipping was built into the product.

Ref: Page 363 of **Pro SQL Server 2005 High Availability**
Log Shipping - **http://msdn2.microsoft.com/en-us/library/aa213785(SQL.80).aspx**

Question 7

What is the registry key to check to see if a server needs a reboot?

Choose one of the answers below:

1. HKEY_LOCAL_MACHINE\SYSTEM\CurrentControlSet\Control\Session Manager\AppPatches\NeedsReboot

2. HKEY_LOCAL_MACHINE\SYSTEM\CurrentControlSet\Control\Session Manager\Power\PendingFileRenameOperations

3. HKEY_LOCAL_MACHINE\SYSTEM\CurrentControlSet\Control\Session Manager\PendingFileRenameOperations

4. HKEY_LOCAL_MACHINE\SYSTEM\CurrentControlSet\Control\Session Manager\Reboot

Answer:

3. HKEY_LOCAL_MACHINE\SYSTEM\
CurrentControlSet\Control\Session
Manager\PendingFileRenameOperations

Explanation:

HKEY_LOCAL_MACHINE\SYSTEM\Curre
ntControlSet\Control\Session
Manager\PendingFileRenameOperations.

Ref: Page 580 of **Pro SQL Server 2005 High Availability**
Incomplete Updates check -
**http://technet.microsoft.com/en-us/library/
bb418921.aspx**

Question 8

If you query the property IsSyncWithBackup, what should the value be if it is not set?

Choose one of the answers below:

1. Sync

2. 1

3. No

4. 0

Answer:

4. 0

Explanation:

If IsSyncWithBackup is not set, the value should be 0.

Ref: Page 580 of **Pro SQL Server 2005 High Availability**
How to: Enable Coordinated Backups for Transactional Replication -
http://technet.microsoft.com/en-us/library/ms147311.aspx

Question 9

Is it possible to modify data in a table variable passed as a PARAMETER to stored procedure in SQL Server 2008?

Choose one of the answers below:

1. Yes

2. No

3. Not possible to pass a table variable as parameter to stored procedure

Answer:

2. No

Explanation:

Table variables are READONLY when passed as a parameter to Stored Procedure. These can be used but not modified. Look for further details at **http://msdn.microsoft.com/en-us/library/ bb510489.aspx**

Question 10

How can you remove the filter created by a CREATE SUBCUBE statement in an MDX query?

Choose one of the answers below:

1. It is removed when the batch ends.

2. Issue the CLEAR SUBCUBE statement.

3. Issue the DROP SUBCUBE statement.

4. Issue the CLEAR FILTER statement.

Answer:

3. Issue the DROP SUBCUBE statement.

Explanation:

After you create a subcube, it is used for all subsequent batches until the DROP SUBCUBE statement is submitted or the session closes.

Ref: Building Subcubes in MDX -
http://msdn2.microsoft.com/en-us/library/ ms144774.aspx

Question 11

In the SQLCMD utility, how can you change your password and then execute a script?

Choose one of the answers below:

1. Use the -P parameter.

2. Use the -N parameter

3. Use the -n parameter

4. Use the -z parameter.

Answer:

4. Use the -z parameter.

Explanation:

By using the -z command, you can submit a new password along with your existing credentials and the script you wish to run. A -Z would change your password and exit.

Ref: sqlcmd utility -
http://msdn2.microsoft.com/en-us/library/ms162773.aspx

Question 12

You need to perform a restore operation as part of a log shipping operation and want to do it quickly from the server. However SSMS is not running correctly on the server. What can you do within the log shipping subsystem?

Choose one of the answers below:

1.   Use the sqllogship.exe command line utility.

2.   Use the logship.exe command line utility.

3.   Use sqlcmd.exe with the -L parameter to indicate log shipping operations and the "restore [id]" command as the script.

4.   Use the sqlcmd.exe application with the appropriate RESTORE command. The log shipping configuration will recognize this is a database involved with log shipping.

Answer:

1. Use the sqllogship.exe command line utility.

Explanation:

The sqllogship.exe application can be used to perform various operations on a log shipping server.

Ref: sqllogship Application -
**http://msdn2.microsoft.com/en-us/library/
bb283327.aspx**

Question 13

What does this return in SQL Server 2005?

SELECT RAND() Random_Number GO 5

Choose one of the answers below:

1. 1 result set with 1 random number

2. 1 result set with 5 random numbers

3. 5 result sets of 1 random number each

4. 5 result sets of 5 random numbers each.

Answer:

3. 5 result sets of 1 random number each

Explanation:

This executes the previous batch 5 times, so 5 result sets with 1 random number each are returned.

Ref: GO - **http://msdn2.microsoft.com/en-us/library/ms188037.aspx**

Question 14

In Reporting Services, can Client-Side reporting services report only on SQL Server 2005 as a data source?

Choose one of the answers below:

1. Yes, only for SQL Server 2005 and above.

2. No, but only versions of SQL Server are supported

3. No, client side reporting can report on any data source

Answer:

3. No, client side reporting can report on any data source

Explanation:

The answer is Client-side reporting can be done on any data source from which data can be gathered into a Dataset.

Ref: Data Sources Supported by Reporting Services - **http://msdn2.microsoft.com/en-us/library/ ms159219.aspx**

Question 15

Which type of export output is not possible from ReportViewer at client-side?

Choose one of the answers below:

1. Excel

2. PDF

3. Word

Answer:

3. Word

Explanation:

ReportViewer cannot export the output of report to a MS Word format file.

Ref: Design Considerations for Report Rendering - **http://msdn2.microsoft.com/en-us/library/ ms156268.aspx**

Question 16

Which .NET framework contains the Report Viewer controls?

Choose one of the answers below:

1. 1.1

2. 2

3. Both

4. Neither

Answer:

4. Neither

Explanation:

ReportViewer is not part of either 1.1 or 2.0 version of .NET Framework. The ReportViewer DLL files must be deployed separately.

Ref: Reporting Services and ReportViewer Controls in Visual Studio - **Reporting Services and ReportViewer Controls in Visual Studio**

Question 17

Can a server-side report can be accessed client-side?

Choose one of the answers below:

1. Yes

2. No

3. Yes, but only if the client is a Windows Form application.

Answer:

1. Yes

Explanation:

Reports hosted at server-side can be easily accessed by varies clients, including Widows Forms, Web Forms & Console application to name few.

Ref: Reporting Services and ReportViewer Controls in Visual Studio - **http://msdn2.microsoft.com/en-us/library/ms345248.aspx**

Question 18

What is the maximum amount of parameters a stored procedure can have?

Choose one of the answers below:

1. 256

2. 1024

3. 2048

4. 2100

Answer:

4. 2100

Explanation:

Yes, it's true. A stored procedure can have 2100 parameters passed into it. Please don't take advantage of this :)

Ref: CREATE PROCEDURE - **http://msdn2.microsoft.com/en-us/library/ms 187926.aspx**

Question 19

In SQL Server 2005, how are the primary and secondary systems in log shipping coupled?

Choose one of the answers below:

1. tightly

2. loosely

Answer:

2. Loosely

Explanation:

The two systems (or more) in a log shipping scenario are loosely coupled. The logs are copied and restored asynchronously.

Ref: Loosely Coupled -
http://en.wikipedia.org/wiki/Loose_coupling
Understanding Log Shipping -
http://msdn2.microsoft.com/en-us/library/ms187103.aspx

Question 20

Which recompilation level supported by SQL Server 2000?

Choose one of the answers below:

1. Statement-level recompilation

2. Batch-level recompilation

3. Statement & Batch level

4. None of the above

Answer:

2. Batch-level recompilation

Explanation:

When a batch is recompiled in SQL Server 2000, all of the statements in the batch are recompiled, not just the one that triggered the recompilation. SQL Server 2005 improves upon this behavior by compiling only the statement that caused the recompilation, not the entire batch. This "statement-level recompilation" feature will improve SQL Server 2005's recompilation behavior when compared to that of SQL Server 2000.

Ref:
http://www.microsoft.com/technet/prodtechnol /sql/2005/recomp.mspx#ETD

Question 21

Within a trigger, how can you tell if a value has altered on a specific column?

Choose one of the answers below:

1. UPDATE(column_name)

2. COLUMNS_UPDATED() with bit flag tests

3. SELECT from UPDATED transient table table found in a trigger

4. a or b

Answer:

4. a or b

Explanation:

You can either use UPDATE(column_name) or COLUMNS_UPDATED() where you test for an update via BIT Flags.

Ref: Pages 436 and 441 Chapter 13 of **Beginning SQL Server 2005 For Developers** UPDATE() - **http://msdn2.microsoft.com/en-us/library/ms187326.aspx** COLUMNS_UPDATED() - **http://msdn2.microsoft.com/en-us/library/ms186329.aspx**

Question 22

Which ranking function would you use to provide an ascending, non-unique ranking number similar to what you see on leader boards such as golf?

Choose one of the answers below:

1. DENSE_RANK

2. RANK

3. NTILE

4. ROW_NUMBER

Answer:

2. RANK

Explanation:

RANK() is the correct function as it will provide the gaps required when two or more results are the same and a jump is required

Ref: Page 418 of Chapter 12 of **Beginning SQL Server 2005 For Developers**
RANK - **http://msdn2.microsoft.com/en-us/library/
ms176102.aspx**

Question 23

Which statement is the fastest method to delete every row in a table?

Choose one of the answers below:

1. TRUNCATE TABLE

2. DELETE FROM table WITH NO LOGGING

3. DROP TABLE

4. DELETE ALL

Answer:

1. TRUNCATE TABLE

Explanation:

TRUNCATE TABLE will delete every row as it does not log every rows deletion in the transaction log

Ref: Page 306 of Chapter 8 of **Beginning SQL Server 2005 For Developers**
TRUNCATE - **http://msdn2.microsoft.com/en-us/library/ms177570.aspx**

Question 24

Which clause would you use when you want to amalgamate data from two tables in to 1 row?

Choose one of the answers below:

1. WHERE

2. JOIN

3. GROUP BY

4. HAVING

Answer:

2. JOIN

Explanation:

You should use the JOIN clause. You may come across usage of the WHERE clause but this should be avoided

Ref: Page 359 of Chapter 11 of **Beginning SQL Server 2005 For Developers**
SELECT - **http://msdn2.microsoft.com/en-us/library/ms176104.aspx**

Question 25

Which functionality provides the best granularity of
ownership of objects within SQL Server?

Choose one of the answers below:

1. create objects with schemas

2. create every object with a specific user
   account

3. create all objects with dbo account

4. create objects with specific prefixes

Answer:

1. Create objects with schemas

Explanation:

Schemas provide developers with the best solution for ownership as objects are not owned by a specific account, so less maintenance is required when users are removed. It also allows grouping of like objects giving developers a greater immediate knowledge of those objects' use.

Ref: Page 111 of Chapter 4 of **Beginning SQL Server 2005 For Developers**
Schemas - **http://msdn2.microsoft.com/en-us/library/ms365789.aspx**

Question 26

Which tool would you use to configure SQL Server 2005 to allow remote connections?

Choose one of the answers below:

1. SQL Server Configuration Manager

2. SQL Server Surface Area Configuration

3. SQL Server Management Studio Express

Answer:

2. SQL Server Surface Area Configuration

Explanation:

To enable remote connections on the instance of SQL Server 2005 and to turn on the SQL Server Browser service, use the SQL Server 2005 Surface Area Configuration tool. The Surface Area Configuration tool is installed when you install SQL Server 2005.

Ref: **http://support.microsoft.com/kb/914277**

Question 27

What will be the output of this query?

RAISERROR ('Invalid Input', 0, 1)

Choose one of the answers below:

1. Invalid Input

2. Msg 50000, Level 16, State 1, Line 1 Invalid Input

3. Msg 2754, Level 16, State 1, Line 1 Error severity levels greater than 18 can only be specified by members of the sysadmin role, using the WITH LOG option.

Answer:

1. Invalid Input

Explanation:

In SQL Server there are certain security level are defined by the system and some that are user defined. Severities 0-9 are user informational messages, which can be errors or just messages.

Ref: Database Engine Error Severities - **http://msdn2.microsoft.com/en-us/library/ms164086.aspx**

Raiserror - **http://msdn2.microsoft.com/en-us/library/ms178592.aspx**

Question 28

What will be the output of this query if run by a normal user?

RAISERROR ('Invalid Input', 20, 1)
GO

Choose one of the answers below:

1. Msg 2754, Level 16, State 1, Line 1Error severity levels greater than 18 can only be specified by members of the sysadmin role, using the WITH LOG option.

2. Msg 170, Level 15, State 1, Line 1 Line 1: Incorrect syntax near ')'.

3. Msg 50000, Level 16, State 1, Line 1 Invalid Input

Answer:

1. Msg 2754, Level 16, State 1, Line 1Error severity levels greater than 18 can only be specified by members of the sysadmin role, using the WITH LOG option.

Explanation:

Only sysadmins can raise severities greater than 18. Therefore this will generate an error.

Ref: Database Engine Error Severities - **http://msdn2.microsoft.com/en-us/library/ms164086.aspx**

Raiserror - **http://msdn2.microsoft.com/en-us/library/ms178592.aspx**

Question 29

You are running a trace of login events on SQL Server 2005 and have included the event class for "Audit Login". How can you use this trace to determine if the logins are from a pooled connection or not?

Choose one of the answers below:

1. Add the ConnStatus column to your trace to see this data.

2. Add the TextData column to your trace and it will be listed as a note

3. Add the Event Subclass to your trace to see this data.

4. You cannot get this information from a trace.

Answer:

3. Add the Event Subclass to your trace to see this data.

Explanation:

If you add the EventSubClass field to the trace, it will display pooled connection status.

Ref: Audit Login Event Class -
Login Events include Pooled Connections -
http://feeds.feedburner.com/~r/SqlteamcomWebl ogs/~3/177719367/Login-Events-include-Pooled- Connections.aspx

Question 30

You have 200 databases on one of your large SQL Servers and want to suppress the "successful backup" messages from being written to your log. How can you do this effectively?

Choose one of the answers below:

1. Stop and restart SQL Server with the "-No_Success" parameter

2. Run SQL Server with trace flag 3226

3. Add the "WITH NO_MSGS" parameter to your backup command.

4. You cannot suppress this information from being written to the log.

Answer:

2. Run SQL Server with trace flag 3226

Explanation:

Trace flag 3226 will suppress the success messages from being written to the SQL Server error log as well as the System Event log.

Ref: Storage Engine Blog - When is too much success a bad thing? - **http://blogs.msdn.com/sqlserverstorageengine/archive/2007/10/30/when-is-too-much-success-a-bad-thing.aspx**

Question 31

When using the OPENROWSET command, how is
the data source accessed?

Choose one of the answers below:

1. Using the DB-Library API

2. Using the OLEDB API

3. Using the ADO.NET API

Answer:

2. Using the OLEDB API

Explanation:

The OPENROWSET command uses the OLEDB providers.

Ref: OPENROWSET -
**http://msdn2.microsoft.com/en-us/library/
ms190312.aspx**

Question 32

If you log in with a SQL Server authenticated account to a SQL Server 2005 instance and use the OPENROWSET command, which security profile is used?

Choose one of the answers below:

1. Your Windows account is impersonated.

2. The profile assigned to your SQL Server login.

3. The security context of the SQL Server service account.

4. The SQL Agent service account security context.

Answer:

3. The security context of the SQL Server service account.

Explanation:

When you log in with a SQL Server authenticated account, the security profile of that particular SQL Server process, usually the service account, is used.

Ref: Importing Bulk Data by Using BULK INSERT or OPENROWSET - **http://msdn2.microsoft.com/en-us/library/ms175915.aspx**

Question 33

You log into a SQL Server 2005 instance with Windows authentication and use the OPENROWSET command to import data. The source data file is located on the local server and while your Windows account does not have read access to the folder, the SQL Server service account does. Can you import the data?

Choose one of the answers below:

1. Yes

2. No

Answer:

2. No

Explanation:

When you log in to SQL Server using Windows authentication and run the OPENROWSET command, only those files that your Windows account can read can be used to import data. The rights of the SQL Server service account are not used.

Ref: Importing Bulk Data by Using BULK INSERT or OPENROWSET - **http://msdn2.microsoft.com/en-us/library/ ms175915.aspx**

Question 34

In which filegroups must the mdf (or first file) file reside in a SQL Server 2005 database?

Choose one of the answers below:

1. Any filegroup

2. The PRIMARY filegroup

3. The SYSTEM filegroup

Answer:

2. The PRIMARY filegroup

Explanation:

The mdf file, the main data file which holds metadata about the database, must reside in the PRIMARY filegroup. This is the first filegroup created with a database and its name cannot be changed.

Ref: Physical Database Files and Filegroups - **http://msdn2.microsoft.com/en-us/library/ms179316.aspx**

Question 35

You are starting a new job and examining your SQL Server 2005 server instances and come across a number of files with the DTSX extension in the SQL Server folders. What are these files used for?

Choose one of the answers below:

1. These are log files from SQL Agent

2. These are DTS packages upgraded from SQL Server 2000

3. These are Integration Services packages

4. These have nothing to do with SQL Server, you can delete them.

Answer:

3. These are Integration Services packages

Explanation:

Integration Services packages are stored with a DTSX extension by default in the file system.

Ref: Save SSIS Package -
http://technet.microsoft.com/en-us/library/ ms186943.aspx

Question 36

On which types of file systems can SQL Server 2005 database files be located? (Choose all the apply)

Choose two of the answers below:

1. FAT

2. NTFS

3. RAW

4. NFS

Answer:

1. FAT
2. NTFS

Explanation:

SQL Server 2005 can locate database and log files on both FAT and NTFS partitions. NTFS is recommended because of security.

Ref: Physical Database Files and Filegroups - **http://msdn2.microsoft.com/en-us/library/ ms179316.aspx**

Question 37

A developer had a hard drive crash and the SQL
Server 2005 database on which he was working had a
number of changed objects that you need to recover.
He does not have a recent back up, but the MDF and
NDF files were on a separate drive and are accessible.
What can you do?

Choose one of the answers below:

1. Create a blank LDF file in Notepad and use
    that to attach.

2. Use the CREATE DATABASE FOR
    ATTACH command

3. Use the CREATE DATABASE FOR
    ATTACH_REBUILD_LOG

4. Use the CREATE DATABASE FOR
    ATTACH WITH NO_LOG command.

Answer:

3. Use the CREATE DATABASE FOR ATTACH_REBUILD_LOG

Explanation:

If you have the data files, you can do a CREATE DATABASE using the FOR_ATTACH_REBUILD_LOG parameter. Note that this breaks your log chain, so a full backup is recommended after this is complete.

Ref: CREATE DATABASE - **http://msdn2.microsoft.com/en-us/library/ms176061.aspx**

Question 38

If you run this query:

select datediff (ms,getdate()-28,getdate())

Which error will be expected?

Choose one of the answers below:

1. Difference of two datetime columns caused overflow at runtime

2. The conversion of a char data type to a datetime data type resulted in an out-of-range datetime value

3. None

Answer:

1. Difference of two datetime columns caused overflow at runtime

Explanation:

This will produce an overflow error.

Ref: **http://www.sql-server-performance.com/faq/difference_of_datetime_columns_caused_overflow_p1.aspx**

Question 39

In AS2005, you have a cube with two measures:
NumOrder (Count of IdOrder field) and
SumInvoicing (Sum of Invoicing field) and one
dimension: TimeAnalysis. You want allow users to
modify OLAP data from Excel, is this possible?

Choose one of the answers below:

1. No, writeback OLAP Data is not allowed in
    AS 2005

2. No, writeback to a count measure is not
    allowed in AS 2005

3. Yes, writeback option can be enabled for this
    cube in AS 2005

4. Yes, but only an Administrator account can
    delete data in AS 2005

Answer:

2. No, writeback to a count measure is not allowed in AS 2005

Explanation:

Writeback cannot be enabled for measure groups that contain aggregate functions other than Sum.

Ref: Write-Enabled Cubes -
http://technet.microsoft.com/en-us/library/ aa216376(SQL.80).aspx

Question 40

Can you use a WHERE clause with TRUNCATE to limit this rows are removed from a table?

Choose one of the answers below:

1. Yes, if you truncate a view

2. Yes, if you truncate an indexed view

3. Yes with any tables

4. No

Answer:

4. No

Explanation:

The TRUNCATE command cannot include a WHERE clause. It removes all the rows from a table.

Ref: Truncate - **http://technet.microsoft.com/en-us/library/ms177570.aspx**

Question 41

What types of locks does TRUNCATE use? (Check all that apply)

Choose two of the answers below:

1. Table

2. Page

3. Row

4. Database

Answer:

1. Table
2. Page

Explanation:

The TRUNCATE command will use table and page locks.

Ref: TRUNCATE -
http://technet.microsoft.com/en-us/library/ms177570.aspx

Question 42

What will this return?

```sql
 DECLARE @nstring nchar(12)   SET @nstring
= N'SQL Server'  SELECT
UNICODE(@nstring),
NCHAR(UNICODE(@nstring))
```

Choose one of the answers below:

1. 1, 'S'

2. 0, 'S'

3. 83, 'SQL Server'

4. 83, 'S'

Answer:

4. 83, 'S'

Explanation:

The Unicode command returns the Unicode value of the first character of the Unicode string passed in.

Ref: UNICODE -
http://technet.microsoft.com/en-us/library/ms180059.aspx

Question 43

You have a column of data that was digitally signed
by a certificate in your SQL Server 2005 database.
The signature for each row is stored in another
column in the same table. How can you be sure that
this data has not been changed?

Choose one of the answers below:

1. If the data is digitally signed, it cannot be
    changed.

2. You can use the VerifySignedByCert function
    to check.

3. You would need to build a CLR function that
    could re-compute the signature and check it
    against what is stored.

4. There is no way to do this.

Answer:

2. You can use the VerifySignedByCert function to check.

Explanation:

If you have the signature, the data, and the certificate, the VerifySignedByCert function can be used to determine if the data is the same.

Ref: VerifySignedByCert -
http://technet.microsoft.com/en-us/library/ms178631.aspx

Question 44

You have a table with 4,294,967,296 rows. You issue an update that should affect all but 3 or 4 rows. You want to determine how many rows were affected by the update. How can you do this?

Choose one of the answers below:

1. Issue SELECT @@@ROWCOUNT

2. Issue SELECT @@@BIGCOUNT

3. Issue SELECT @@@ROWCOUNT_BIG

4. Issue SELECT ROWCOUNT_BIG()

Answer:

4. Issue SELECT ROWCOUNT_BIG()

Explanation:

The @@rowcount variable is an INT and can only count rows up to $2^{31} - 1$. To get a larger rowcount, you would need to use the ROWCOUNT_BIG() function.

Ref: ROWCOUNT_BIG() - **http://technet.microsoft.com/en-us/library/ms181406.aspx**

Question 45

Assuming both the objects exists, what would be the output of the below query.

SELECT *   FROM dbo.Customers MIDDLE JOIN dbo.Employees ON CustomerID = EmployeeID

Choose one of the answers below:

1. Incorrect syntax near keyword JOIN

2. Join predicate MIDDLE is invalid in this context

3. A resultset with columns will be returned

Answer:

3. A resultset with columns will be returned

Explanation:

MIDDLE is not a keyword or a join predicate in SQL. In this case, the optimizer treats MIDDLE as the alias name for table Customers. And also the join type [INNER/OUTER/CROSS] is optional and if not specified, will defaults to INNER JOIN.

Question 46

How many types of DML triggers in SQL are present? (DML - Data Modification Language)

Choose one of the answers below:

1. 1 type (DML triggers)

2. 3 types (DML triggers, DDL triggers and Logon triggers)

3. 2 types (AFTER trigger and INSTEAD OF trigger)

4. 4 types (AFTER Trigger, FOR trigger, CLR trigger and INSTEAD OF trigger)

Answer:

3. 2 types (AFTER trigger and INSTEAD OF trigger)

Explanation:

There are only two types of DML triggers present. AFTER and INSTEAD OF, we normally use FOR as a keyword to define a trigger but it comes under the AFTER trigger and it performs the same action as after trigger do.

For further clarification see this link **http://msdn2.microsoft.com/en-us/library/ ms178134.aspx** this link also contains CLR Triggers but they can also be a DDL trigger that is why they cannot be count under the pur DML triggers category.

Question 47

What is a domain in SQL Server database design?

Choose one of the answers below:

1. All the instances on a server

2. All the values for a field

3. All the logins on an instance

4. A group of SQL Servers.

Answer:

2. All the values for a field

Explanation:

A domain in SQL Server database design, or any database design or modelling, is the list of possible values for a particular field. This may be a technical or business listing.
For example, the domain of values for a tinyint field is the list of values from 0 to 127. For a gender field, it might be Male or Female, or possibly other values.

Ref: Domain -
http://databases.about.com/cs/administration/g/domain.htm

Question 48

By default when you install SQL Server 2005 Standard or Enterprise, which protocols are enabled? (Check all that apply)

Choose two of the answers below:

1. TCP/IP

2. Named Pipes

3. Shared Memory

4. VIA

Answer:

1. TCP/IP
3. Shared Memory

Explanation:

By default, the TCP/IP and Shared Memory protocols are enabled.

Ref: Network Protocols and Network Libraries - **http://msdn2.microsoft.com/en-us/library/ ms143671.aspx**

Question 49

How many network protocols are available on SQL Server 2005?

Choose one of the answers below:

1. 1

2. 2

3. 3

4. 4

5. 5

Answer:

4. 4

Explanation:

The protocols available in SQL Server 2005 are TCP/IP, Shared Memory, Named Pipes, and VIA.

Ref: Network Protocols and Network Libraries - **Network Protocols and Network Libraries**

Question 50

You are considering using SQL Server 2005 for your large ERP implementation and your boss wants to install SQL Server 2005 Evaluation Edition on an 8-CPU server. What is the maximum number of processors supported by the Evaluation Edition?

Choose one of the answers below:

1. 1

2. 2

3. 4

4. The Operating System Maximum

Answer:

4. The Operating System Maximum

Explanation:

The number of processors supported by SQL Server 2005 Evaluation Edition is the operating system maximum.

Ref: Maximum Number of Processors Supported by the Editions of SQL Server 2005 - **Maximum Number of Processors Supported by the Editions of SQL Server 2005**

Question 51

You are considering installing SQL Server 2005 Workgroup Edition for your 4 person accounting department to run their Dynamics package on. How many CPUs does Workgroup Edition support?

Choose one of the answers below:

1. 1

2. 2

3. 4

4. Operating System Maximum

Answer:

2. 2

Explanation:

The number of processors supported by SQL Server 2005 Workgroup Edition is 2.

Ref: Maximum Number of Processors Supported by the Editions of SQL Server 2005 - **http://msdn2.microsoft.com/en-us/library/ ms143760.aspx**

Question 52

From which of the following SQL Server editions can you upgrade to SQL Server 2005 Standard Edition?

Choose two of the answers below:

1. SQL Server 7.0 Standard Edition SP3

2. SQL Server 7.0 Standard Edition SP4

3. SQL Server 2000 Standard Edition SP1

4. SQL Server 2000 Standard Edition SP2

5. SQL Server 2000 Standard Edition SP3

Answer:

2. SQL Server 7.0 Standard Edition SP4
5. SQL Server 2000 Standard Edition SP3

Explanation:

The upgrade paths for SQL Server 2005 Standard require the Standard or Workgroup editions of SQL Server previous versions and require SP4 for SQL Server 7 and SP3 for SQL Server 2000.

Ref: Installation Options -
http://msdn2.microsoft.com/en-us/library/ ms143689.aspx

Question 53

If you do not specify a size during CAST and
CONVERT options, what is the default length for
the CHAR data type?

Choose one of the answers below:

1. 4

2. 10

3. 30

4. 50

5. 80

Answer:

3. 30

Explanation:

The default length for cast and convert operations is 30 characters for the CHAR data type.

Ref: Char and varchar -
http://msdn2.microsoft.com/en-us/library/ms143689.aspx

Question 54

Can you run a differential backup on a database in the Simple recovery mode?

Choose one of the answers below:

1. Yes

2. No

Answer:

1. Yes

Explanation:

Yes, you can run a differential backup on a database in the simple recovery mode.

Ref: Backup Under the Simple Recovery Model - **http://msdn2.microsoft.com/en-us/library /ms191164.aspx**

Question 55

If you choose to export data in the native format with the BCP utility, into which of the following systems can you import it with BCP?

Choose one of the answers below:

1. SQL Server

2. Access

3. Oracle

4. Any OLE DB data source

Answer:

1. SQL Server

Explanation:

The native format of bcp can only be used between instances of SQL Server.

Ref: Using Native, Character, or Unicode Formats - **http://msdn2.microsoft.com/en-us/library/ ms188293.aspx**

Question 56

In SQL Server 2005, what does the Replication Log
Reader Agent do?

Choose one of the answers below:

1. This agent monitors the publication
   transaction log and sends new records to the
   distribution database.

2. This agent monitors the distribution
   transaction log and sends new records to the
   subscription database(s).

3. This agent monitors the subscriber activity to
   ensure they are receiving data.

4. There is no such agent.

Answer:

1. This agent monitors the publication transaction log and sends new records to the distribution database.

Explanation:

The replication log reader agent monitors the publication transaction log and copies the appropriate records to the distribution database.

Ref: Replication Log Reader Agent - **http://msdn2.microsoft.com/en-us/library/ ms146878.aspx**

Question 57

What does the replication Merge Agent do? (Check all that apply)

Choose two of the answers below:

1. Applies the initial snapshot to the subscribers

2. Reconciles data issues at the publisher in merge replication

3. Reconciles data issues at the subscriber in merge replication

4. Reads the subscriber transaction log to determine if changes need to be applied.

Answer:

1. Applies the initial snapshot to the subscribers
2. Reconciles data issues at the publisher in merge replication

Explanation:

The replication merge agent handles the initial snapshots on the subscribers (applying) managing changes at the publisher, and reconciling conflicts at the publisher.

Ref: Replication Merge Agent -
http://msdn2.microsoft.com/en-us/library/ms147839.aspx

Question 58

If you wish to write a .NET application using the management framework to manage your SQL Server 2005 replication setup, which set of objects would you use?

Choose one of the answers below:

1. SMO

2. RMO

3. XAML

4. XRML

Answer:

2. RMO

Explanation:

Replication Management Objects (RMO) are used to programmatically work with replication.

Ref: Replication Management Objects - **http://msdn2.microsoft.com/en-us/library/ms148076.aspx**

Question 59

From where does the replication queue reader agent get its data?

Choose one of the answers below:

1. The publisher transaction log

2. The distributor transaction log

3. From the distribution database

4. From a message queue

Answer:

4. From a message queue

Explanation:

The replication queue reader agent reads data from a message queue when you implement transactional replication with queued updates.

Ref: Replication Queue Reader Agent-
http://msdn2.microsoft.com/en-us/library/ms147378.aspx

Question 60

Which of these objects are published in transactional replication? (Choose all that apply)

Choose four of the answers below:

1. Partitioned Tables

2. CLR Stored Procedures

3. CLR Data Types

4. Full test indexes

Answer:

1. Partitioned Tables
2. CLR Stored Procedures
3. CLR Data Types
4. Full test indexes

Explanation:

All of these objects are published in transactional
replication.
Ref: Publishing Data and Database Objects -
**http://msdn2.microsoft.com/en-us/library/
ms152559.aspx**

Question 61

What is a surrogate key?

Choose one of the answers below:

1. A primary key derived from application data

2. A primary key not derived from application data

3. A secondary foreign key to a parent table.

4. There is no such thing.

Answer:

2. A primary key not derived from application data

Explanation:

A surrogate key is a key that is artificially created to uniquely identify each row in a database. It is not derived from the application data stored in the database.

Ref: Surrogate Key - **http://en.wikipedia.org/wiki/Surrogate_key**

Question 62

Cryptography in SQL Server is essentially made of:
(Check all that apply)

Choose four of the answers below:

1. Symmetric key processing

2. Asymmetric key processing

3. One-way hashing

4. A hybrid approach of two or more of the above.

5. Only symmetric and asymmetric key processing.

Answer:

1. Symmetric key processing
2. Asymmetric key processing
3. One-way hashing
4. A hybrid approach of two or more of the above.

Explanation:

Cryptography in SQL Server is essentially made of
Symmetric key processing, Asymmetric key
processing, One-way hashing or a hybrid approach of
one or more of the above.
Ref: Encryption Hierarchy -
**http://msdn.microsoft.com/en-us/library/
ms189586.aspx**

Question 63

In Service Broker, if your message does not send and has an error, where do you find this error?

Choose one of the answers below:

1. In sys.transmission_queue.is_conversation _error

2. In sys.transmission_queue.transmission _status

3. In sys.service_broker.errors

4. In sys.service_broker.transmission_error

Answer:

2. In sys.transmission_queue.transmission_status

Explanation:

The error message for a message that is unable to be delivered in Service Broker is often held in the sys.transmission_queue.transmissions_status field.

Ref: sys.transmission_queue -
http://msdn2.microsoft.com/en-us/library/ms190336.aspx

Question 64

What does EOIO mean in Service Broker messaging?

Choose one of the answers below:

1. Every Object Is Ordered

2. Each Object In Order

3. Exactly Once In Order

4. Every Other Is Open

Answer:

3. Exactly Once In Order

Explanation:

Service Broker provides reliable message service with each message delivered once in the proper order, so this means: exactly once in order.

Ref: Dialog Conversations - **http://msdn2.microsoft.com/en-us/library/ ms166083.aspx**

Question 65

Which command is used to back up your Database
Master Key?

Choose one of the answers below:

1. BACKUP DATABASE KEY

2. BACKUP MASTER KEY

3. BACKUP KEY

4. BACKUP SERVICE MASTER KEY

Answer:

2. BACKUP MASTER KEY

Explanation:

The correct commend for backing up the Database Master Key is BACKUP MASTER KEY.

Ref: BACKUP MASTER KEY - **http://msdn2.microsoft.com/en-us/library/ ms174387.aspx**

Question 66

What does GETANSINULL return the nullability of?

Choose one of the answers below:

1. A database

2. A column

3. A table

4. A schema

Answer:

1. A database

Explanation:

The GETANSINULL function returns the nullability of a database.

Ref: GETANSINULL -
http://msdn2.microsoft.com/en-us/library/ms174960.aspx

Question 67

Which DMV would you query in SQL Server 2005 for index fragmentation?

Choose one of the answers below:

1. sys.dm_db_index_operational_stats

2. sys.dm_db_index_physical_stats

3. sys.dm_db_index_usage_stats

4. sys.dm_db_index_fragmentation_issues

Answer:

2. sys.dm_db_index_physical_stats

Explanation:

The sys.dm_db_index_physical_stats DMV will show fragmentation in your indexes.

Ref: sys.dm_db_index_physical_stats - **http://msdn2.microsoft.com/en-us/library/ms188917.aspx**

Question 68

Which version of SQL Server will RTM this year?

Choose one of the answers below:

1. Hydra

2. Katmai

3. Sphinx

4. Yukon

Answer:

2. Katmai

Explanation:

SQL Server 2008, AKA Katmai, will RTM in 2008.

Ref: SQL Server Code Names -
**http://en.wikipedia.org/wiki/Microsoft_codenam
es#SQL_Server_family**

Question 69

Can you use TOP with any UPDATE statement?

Choose one of the answers below:

1. Yes

2. No, it cannot be used with partitioned views

3. No, it cannot be used with any UPDATE
   statement

Answer:

2. No, it cannot be used with partitioned views

Explanation:

The TOP command can be used with UPDATE statements, except where a partitioned view is being updated.

Ref: TOP - **http://msdn2.microsoft.com/en-us/library/ms189463.aspx**

Question 70

If you run "sqlwb mysql.sql" from the command line, what happens?

Choose one of the answers below:

1. An error because there is no hyphen "-" before the file

2. SSMS opens and brings up mysql.sql in a query window.

3. SSMS opens and executes mysql.sql in a query window against the default database

4. SSMS opens and ignores the parameter.

Answer:

2. SSMS opens and brings up mysql.sql in a query window.

Explanation:

sqlwb is the executable for SQL Server Management Studio. If you pass the path and name of a file, it will be opened in a query window when SSMS starts.

Ref: SSMS switches - **http://blogs.msdn.com/buckwoody/archive/2007/11/29/go-get-me-a-switch.aspx**

Question 71

Will your SQL-DMO applications work with SQL
Server 2005?

Choose one of the answers below:

1. Yes

2. No

Answer:

1. Yes

Explanation:

SQL Server 2005 still supports SQL-DMO applications; however this framework will be deprecated in SQL Server 2008.

Ref: Backward Compatibility with SQL Server 2000 Tools- **http://msdn2.microsoft.com/en-us/library /ms174190.aspx**

Question 72

In SQL Server 2005, what is the default interval between checkpoints?

Choose one of the answers below:

1. 1 minute

2. 2 minutes

3. 5 minutes

4. SQL Server dynamically manages the interval

Answer:

4. SQL Server dynamically manages the interval

Explanation:

The default setting for the checkpoint interval in SQL Server 2005 is 0, which means the interval is dynamically managed.

Ref: Checkpoint - **http://msdn2.microsoft.com/en-us/library/ms188748.aspx**

Question 73

Which of these operations comes first during recovery?

Choose one of the answers below:

1. Roll Forward

2. Roll Back

Answer:

1. Roll Forward

Explanation:

When the recovery process proceeds, roll forward precedes roll back.

Ref: Understanding How Restore and Recovery of Backups Work in SQL Server - **http://msdn2.microsoft.com/en-us/library/ms191455 .aspx**

Question 74

What is the maximum storage capacity of XML data type?

Choose one of the answers below:

1. 4 GB

2. 2 GB

3. UNLIMITED

Answer:

2. 2 GB

Explanation:

There is a 2GB limit on the XML datatype.

Ref: Maximum Capacity Specifications for SQL
Server 2005 - **http://msdn2.microsoft.com/en-
us/library/ms143432.aspx**

Question 75

What is the maximum size of the session context information in SQL Server 2000?

Choose one of the answers below:

1. 32 bytes

2. 64 bytes

3. 128 bytes

4. 256 bytes

Answer:

3. 128 bytes

Explanation:

SQL Server 2000 allows associations of up to 128 bytes of binary information with the current session or connection using SET CONTEXT_INFO.

Ref: SET CONTEXT_INFO -
http://technet.microsoft.com/en-us/library/ ms187768.aspx

Question 76

If you create a view in SQL Server 2005 without schemabinding, such as

CREATE VIEW myview as   select * from MyTable

and the schema of MyTable changes, what can you do to refresh the view and see the schema changes?

Choose one of the answers below:

1. Run sp_refreshview

2. Run ALTER VIEW myview REFRESH

3. Run ALTER VIEW myview UPDATE_METADATA

4. You have to drop and recreate the view

Answer:

1. Run sp_refreshview

Explanation:

The sp_refreshview system stored procedure will update the metadata of the view with changes to the underlying tables.

Ref: sp_refreshview -
**http://msdn2.microsoft.com/en-
us/library/ms187821
.aspx**

Question 77

Which version of Windows supports Hot Add CPUs for SQL Server 2008? (Check all that apply)

Choose two of the answers below:

1. Windows Server 2008 Datacenter Edition x64

2. Windows Server 2008 Datacenter Edition x86 and x64

3. Any Windows Server 2008 edition

4. Windows Server 2008 Enterprise Edition x64

Answer:

1. Windows Server 2008 Datacenter Edition x64
4. Windows Server 2008 Enterprise Edition x64

Explanation:

Hot-add CPUs require the 64-bit edition of Windows Server 2008 Datacenter or the Windows Server 2008 Enterprise Edition for Itanium-Based Systems operating system.

Ref: Hot Add CPU -
http://technet.microsoft.com/en-us/library/ bb964703(SQL.100).aspx

Question 78

What does the status column that is returned from sp_helpdb mean in SQL Server 2005?

Choose one of the answers below:

1. The online/offline/restoring status?

2. The options set on the database

3. It returns a 1 if the database is corrupt

4. This shows a 1 if there are users connected to the database.

Answer:

2. The options set on the database

Explanation:

The status column from sp_helpdb shows a comma delimited list of the options set on a database.

Ref: Sp_helpdb - **http://msdn2.microsoft.com/en-us/library/ms178568.aspx**

Question 79

What does sp_validname do?

Choose one of the answers below:

1. Checks if a parameter passed in is a valid SQL Server identifier

2. Generates a valid, but random, object identifier

3. Removes invalid characters from an identifier passed in.

4. Automatically adds brackets ([]) to an identifier.

Answer:

1. Checks if a parameter passed in is a valid SQL Server identifier

Explanation:

The sp_validname procedure checks if a parameter passed in is a valid identifier.

Ref: sp_validname -
http://msdn2.microsoft.com/en-us/library/ms189525.aspx

Question 80

When someone accesses a view, which settings for ANSI_NULLS and QUOTE_IDENTIFIER are used?

Choose one of the answers below:

1. The server settings at the time the query is run.

2. The client (session) settings at the time the query is run.

3. The server settings when the view was created.

4. The client (session) settings when the view was created.

Answer:

4. The client (session) settings when the view was created.

Explanation:

The settings that were set when the view was created (for the session) are used.

Ref: CREATE VIEW -
http://msdn2.microsoft.com/en-us/library/ms189525.aspx

Question 81

In peer to peer replication, each node

Choose one of the answers below:

1. Subscribes to a subset of schema and data

2. Subscribes to the same schema and a subset of data

3. Subscribes to the same schema and data

4. Subscribes to a subset of the schema and all the data

Answer:

3. Subscribes to the same schema and data

Explanation:

Each node is a peer and subscribes to the same schema and data. In this way, all data is available on all nodes and changes made on any node are replicated to all others.

Ref: Peer-to-Peer Transactional Replication - **http://msdn2.microsoft.com/en-us/library/ms151196.aspx**

Question 82

You have a synonym in SQL Server 2005 named "MyTable" for the Sales table. What will happen if you execute this statement, assuming the column does not exists?

ALTER TABLE MyTable ADD NewColumn int

Choose one of the answers below:

1. A new column will be added to the Sales table and visible in the synonym

2. A new column will be added to the Sales table and NOT visible in the synonym

3. An error will occur.

Answer:

3. An error will occur.

Explanation:

A synonym can only be used to reference objects in DML statements, not DDL statements.

Ref: Using Synonyms -
http://msdn2.microsoft.com/en-us/library/ ms190626.aspx

Question 83

In SQL Server 2005, can you reference a synonym located on a linked server from your local server?

Choose one of the answers below:

1. Yes

2. No

Answer:

2. No

Explanation:

Synonyms located on a remote linked server cannot be referenced locally.

Ref: Using Synonyms - **http://msdn2.microsoft.com/en-us/library/ms190626.aspx**

Question 84

In SQL Server 2005, are synonyms schema bound?

Choose one of the answers below:

1. Yes

2. Only if you specify this option when you create them.

3. No

Answer:

3. No

Explanation:

Synonyms are not schema bound, therefore, they cannot be referenced in a number of constraints like rules, defaults, and others.

Ref: Using Synonyms -
http://msdn2.microsoft.com/en-us/library/ms190626.aspx

Question 85

Which versions of SQL Server 2008 will support Hot-Add CPUs?

Choose one of the answers below:

1. 32-bit SQL Server 2008

2. 64-bit SQL Server 2008

Answer:

2. 64-bit SQL Server 2008

Explanation:

Hot-Add CPUs require the 64-bit version of SQL Server 2008.

Ref: SQL Server 2008 Performance and Scale - **http://download.microsoft.com/download/a/c/d/a cd8e043-d69b-4f09-bc9e-4168b65aaa71/SQL2008 PerfandScale.doc**

Question 86

Which versions of SQL Server 2008 support hot-add
memory?

Choose two of the answers below:

1.   32-bit SQL Server 2008

2.   64-bit SQL Server 2008

Answer:

1. 32-bit SQL Server 2008
2. 64-bit SQL Server 2008

Explanation:

Both the 32 and 64 bit versions of SQL Server 2008 will support hot-add memory. You must have the enterprise edition and hardware that supports this as well as AWE enabled for 32-bit system.

Ref: SQL Server 2008 Performance and Scale - **http://download.microsoft.com/download/a/c/d/a cd8e043-d69b-4f09-bc9e-4168b65aaa71/SQL2008 PerfandScale.doc**

Question 87

In SQL 2005 Integration Services can an OLE DB connection be dynamically changed during execution?

Choose one of the answers below:

1. No - In SSIS connections can not be dynamically updated.

2. No - In SSIS connections can only be updated at run time using package configurations.

3. Yes - In SSIS connections can be dynamically updated during execution using package configurations.

4. Yes - In SSIS connections can be dynamically updated during execution using the DTS.Connections collection.

Answer:

4. Yes - In SSIS connections can be dynamically updated during execution using the DTS.Connections collection.

Explanation:

The connection string property of the connection object can be modified during the execution of a SSIS package. It can be reached by using the DTS.Connections collection.

Ref: Managing Packages Programmatically - **http://msdn2.microsoft.com/en-us/library/aa337077.aspx**

Question 88

In the SSIS Slowly Changing Dimension wizard, which change type do we need to choose for implementing SCD type 2 on a dimension column?

Choose one of the answers below:

1. **Historical Attribute**

2. **Fixed Attribute**

3. **Changing Attribute**

4. **Type 2 Attribute**

Answer:

1. Historical Attribute

Explanation:

The Changing Attribute change type is for SCD type 1 (overwriting existing values), and Historical Attribute is for SCD type 2 (preserving historical values by writing the new values into new records). We choose Fixed Attribute when we want to treat changes as error. There is no change type called Type 2 Attribute in SSIS SCD Wizard.

Ref: Chapter 8, Page 258-259.
Slowly Changing Dimension Transformation -
**http://msdn2.microsoft.com/en-us/library/
ms141715.aspx**

Question 89

In SQL Server 2005, we can compose an MDX query
using a graphical user interface (GUI) and then we
can view the resulting MDX statement. Where in
SQL Server can we do this? (MDX query is a select
statement to query data from a cube)

Choose one of the answers below:

1. Analysis Services

2. Integration Services

3. Reporting Services

4. Management Studio

Answer:

3. Reporting Services

Explanation:

In Reporting Services we can create a report that takes data from a cube (Multidimensional Database Report) without having to write an MDX query. Instead, we can use a GUI to select the measure and dimension attribute that we want to include in the report, as well as for specifying the filter criteria. We can view the MDX by clicking the Data tab, and click the … button next to the Dataset drop-down list.

In an Analysis Services project and in Management Studio we can browse the cube using GUI but there is no facility to view the resulting MDX statement. In Integration Services we have Analysis Services Execute DDL task, but there is no facility to query a cube using MDX or GUI. Analysis Services DDL statements are used for creating, dropping, or altering multidimensional objects such as cubes and dimensions.

Ref: Chapter 11, Page 363-365.
Defining Report Datasets -
http://msdn2.microsoft.com/en-us/library/ms156288(SQL.100).aspx

Question 90

In data warehousing, what term is normally used for calling a data store that is used for transforming and preparing the data obtained from the source system, before the data is loaded into other data store in a data warehouse?

Choose one of the answers below:

1. Stage

2. ODS

3. DDS

4. NDS

Answer:

1. Stage

Explanation:

"A stage is an internal data store in the form of file system or database(s) used for transforming and preparing the data obtained from the source systems, before the data is loaded to other data stores in a data warehouse". An operational data store (ODS) is a hybrid data store in the form of one or more normalized relational databases, containing the transaction data and the most recent version of master data, for the purpose of supporting operational applications. "A dimensional data store (DDS) is a user-facing data store, in the form of one or more relational databases, where the data is arranged in dimensional format for the purpose of supporting analytical queries". A normalized data store (NDS) is an internal master data store in the form of one or more normalized relational databases for the purpose of integrating data from various source systems captured in a stage, before the data is loaded to a user-facing data store.

Ref: Chapter 2, Page 30.Data Preparation Area - **http://msdn2.microsoft.com/en-us/library/ aa905985(sql.80).aspx**

Question 91

Which one of the following is not master data?

Choose one of the answers below:

1. Destination

2. Purchase Order

3. Account

4. Risk

Answer:

2. Purchase Order

Explanation:

Transaction data consists of business entities in OLTP systems that record business transactions/events, consisting of identity, attribute and value columns. Sales order and purchase order are examples of transaction data. Master data consists of the business entities in the OLTP systems that describe business transactions, consisting of identity and attribute columns. Destination is master data used primarily in travel industry; it denotes an end-point of a trip, usually a name of a city, an island or a country. Account is master data widely used in financial industry (such as bank account) and in utility and telco industry (such as customer account). Risk is a master data used in insurance industry; it is the entity or subject which a policy covers.

Ref: Chapter 1, Page 20-21.
Data Integration Solutions for Master Data Management - **http://msdn2.microsoft.com/en-us/library/aa964123.aspx**

Question 92

There are many things that we can use to improve data warehouse performance. Which one of the following things that is not usually used to improve data warehouse query performance?

Choose one of the answers below:

1. Summary Tables

2. Horizontal table partitioning

3. Indexing

4. Backup

Answer:

4. Backup

Explanation:

Summary tables are used to store aggregate data. They improve the query performance because the answers to users queries are already pre-calculated.
Horizontal table partitioning is splitting a table horizontally into several smaller tables, with each table containing some rows of the original table. The nature of the fact tables in dimensional data warehouses is that their content is chronological according to time. Partitioning fact table data warehouse by date makes the query faster because it only needs to get data from certain partitions rather than from the whole table. This is particularly useful for periodic snapshot fact tables. Indexing improves query performance because it provide direct access path to the data. Indexing is particularly useful when querying large tables containing multi-million rows. For example, indexes on the fact table dimensional key columns can improve the dimensional query performance significantly.
Backup is a copy of a database, usually created periodically, to be restored to the original database in the case of disaster or other events. Backup doesn't affect query performance.

Ref: Chapter 6, Page 161-170. Tuning Data Warehouse Performance - **http://msdn2.microsoft.com/en-us/library/aa906007(sql.80).aspx**

Question 93

In the new MERGE syntax, which clause contains the "new" data to be inserted?

**MERGE Address AS NewAddress Using (
SELECT CustomerID, Address1, address2
FROM Customers) AS source(CustomerID, address1, address2) ON
(NewAddress.customerID =
source.CustomerID) WHEN NOT MATCHED THEN
INSERT (CustomerID, Address1, address)
VALUES (source.CustomerID,
source.address1, source.address2 WHEN MATCHED THENUPDATE SET address1 =
source.address1, address2 = source.address2**

Choose one of the answers below:

1. USING

2. ON

3. WHEN MATCHED

4. WHEN NOT MATCHED

Answer:

1. USING

Explanation:

The USING clause of the MERGE statement contains the new data that is being merged into an existing table.

Ref: Merge - **http://msdn2.microsoft.com/en-us/library/bb510625(SQL.100).aspx**

Question 94

Which type of language is a GRANT statement considered?

Choose one of the answers below:

1. DDL

2. DML

3. DCL

4. TCL

Answer:

3. DCL

Explanation:

A Grant statement is considered a data control language (DCL) statement.

Ref: SQL Data Control Language -
http://en.wikipedia.org/wiki/SQL#Data_control

Question 95

What does the DUMP command do?

Choose one of the answers below:

1. Truncates the transaction log

2. Backs up a database or log

3. Clears the error log and starts a new one

4. Clears the data cache.

Answer:

2. Backs up a database or log

Explanation:

Dump is included for backwards compatibility. It can perform a database or log backup.

Ref: Dump - **http://msdn2.microsoft.com/en-us/library/ms187315.aspx**

Question 96

Given the following table variable definition:

DECLARE @Vendors TABLE (VendorPK int, VendorName varchar(50), VendorStatus char(1))

Which of the following are NOT valid statements?

Choose two of the answers below:

1. TRUNCATE TABLE @Vendors

2. BEGIN TRANSACTION; INSERT INTO @Vendors VALUES (1, 'Wicked Widgets Inc.', 'A'); ROLLBACK TRANSACTION

3. CREATE INDEX IX_VendorName ON @Vendors (VendorName)

4. INSERT INTO @Vendors VALUES (1, 'Wicked Widgets Inc.', 'A')

Answer:

1. TRUNCATE TABLE @Vendors
3. CREATE INDEX IX_VendorName ON
@Vendors (VendorName)

Explanation:

Although table variables can be used in most places where temporary or real tables can be used there are some exceptions. In this case, the TRUNCATE TABLE and CREATE INDEX statements will result in an error. Table variables do not honor TRANSACTION statements, but putting them in a transaction does not result in an error.

See also: **http://msdn2.microsoft.com/en-us/library/ms175010.aspx**

Question 97

How many times does a User Defined Function (UDF) execute in a given T-SQL query?

Choose one of the answers below:

1. It executes only once.

2. It executes once per row.

3. It executes only once if the UDF is in the FROM clause and executes once per row if it is located in any other clause of the query.

4. It executes once per row if the UDF is in the FROM clause and executes only once if it is located in any other clause of the query.

Answer:

3. It executes only once if the UDF is in the FROM clause and executes once per row if it is located in any other clause of the query.

Explanation:

A UDF will execute once per row if it is located in the column list of a Select statement or the WHERE, HAVING, GROUP BY, or ORDER BY of a T-SQL Select query. It will also execute once per row in the SET clause of an UPDATE statement, the VALUES clause of an INSERT statement, and any time the function is used in a CHECK / DEFAULT constraint or computed columns. If, however, a UDF is in the FROM clause of a SELECT statement, it will execute only once for the entire query.

References: "Designing Database Solutions by using SQL Server 2005 Self-Paced Training Kit" by Microsoft Press, Chapter 6, pgs 173-174.

Question 98

The new hierarchyID in SQL Server 2008 is what data type?

Choose one of the answers below:

int

5. varchar

6. nvarchar

7. CLR data type

Answer:

4. CLR data type

Explanation:

The heirarchyID is a system data type available in SQL Server 2008 to represent hierarchies. It is based on a CLR data type, but is always available, whether the CLR is enabled or not.

Ref: hierarchyID - **http://msdn2.microsoft.com/en-us/library/bb677290(SQL.100).aspx**

Question 99

In a hierarchy using the new hierarchyID data type, if you have two nodes, i and j, what would i<j represent?

Choose one of the answers below:

1. The value of node i is less than that of j

2. In a depth-first traversal, node i comes before node j

3. In distance pathing, i is closer to the root than j

4. i is less deep in the tree than j

Answer:

2. In a depth-first traversal, node i comes before node j

Explanation:

Indexes on hierarchyID data types are in depth-first order, and nodes close to each other in a depth-first traversal are stored near each other.

Ref: Using hierarchyID Data Types -
http://msdn2.microsoft.com/en-us/library/bb677173(SQL.100).aspx

Question 100

What would be the out put of the below script?

```
  CREATE TABLE #myTable (column1 text);
GO  INSERT INTO #myTable VALUES ('test');
GO  SELECT BINARY_CHECKSUM(*) from
#myTable;  GO  DROP TABLE #myTable  GO
```

Choose one of the answers below:

1. Return a int value

2. Error in binarychecksum. There are no
    comparable columns in the binarychecksum
    input.

3. We cannot use Binary Checksum with
    temporary tables

Answer:

2. Error in binarychecksum. There are no comparable columns in the binarychecksum input.

Explanation:

BINARY_CHECKSUM ignores columns of noncomparable data types in its computation. Noncomparable data types include text, ntext, image, cursor, xml, and noncomparable common language runtime (CLR) user-defined types.

Ref: Binary_checksum - **http://msdn.microsoft.com/en-us/library/ms173784.aspx**

SQL Tools
from Red Gate Software

SQL Backup   from $295

Compress, encrypt and monitor SQL Server backups

- ↗ Compress database backups by **up to 95%** for faster backups and restores
- ↗ Protect your data with up to 256-bit AES encryption (SQL Backup Pro only)
- ↗ Monitor your data with an interactive timeline, so you can check and edit the status of past, present and future backup activities
- ↗ Optimize backup performance with multiple threads in SQL Backup's engine

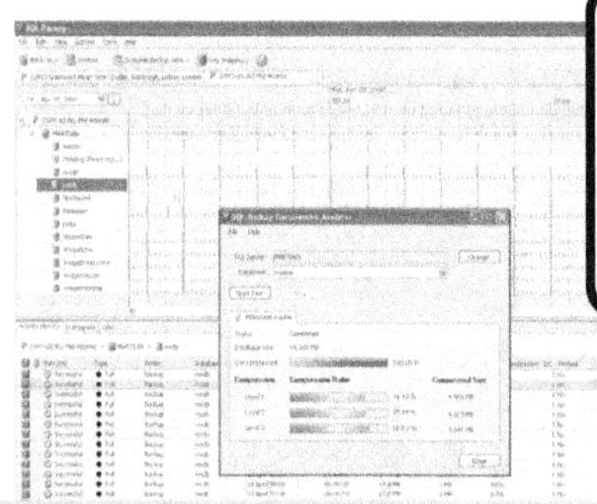

> **"The software has by far the most user-friendly, intuitive interface in its class; the backup routines are well-compressed, encrypted for peace of mind and are transported to our server rapidly. I couldn't be happier."**
> **Kieron Williams** IT Manager, Brunning & Price

SQL Response   from $495

Monitors SQL Servers, with alerts and diagnostic data

- ↗ Investigate long-running queries, SQL deadlocks, blocked processes and more to resolve problems sooner
- ↗ Intelligent email alerts notify you as problems arise, without overloading you with information
- ↗ Concise, relevant data provided for each alert raised
- ↗ Low-impact monitoring and no installation of components on your SQL Servers

> **"SQL Response enables you to monitor, get alerted and respond to SQL problems before they start, in an easy-to-navigate, user-friendly and visually precise way, with drill-down detail where you need it most."**
> **H John B Manderson** President and Principle Consultant, Wireless Ventures Ltd

SQL Prompt   from $195

Intelligent code completion and layout for SQL Server

↗ Write SQL fast and accurately with code completion
↗ Understand code more easily with script layout
↗ Continue to use your current editor – SQL Prompt works within SSMS,
  Query Analyzer, and Visual Studio
↗ Keyword formatting, join completion, code snippets, and many more
  powerful features

> "It's amazing how such a simple concept quickly becomes a way of life. With SQL Prompt there's no longer any need to hunt out the design documentation, or to memorize every field length in the entire database. It's about freeing the mind from being a database repository - and instead concentrate on problem solving and solution providing!" **Dr Michael Dye** Dyetech

SQL Data Generator $295

Test data generator for SQL Server databases

↗ Data generation in one click
↗ Realistic data based on column and table name
↗ Data can be customized if desired
↗ Eliminates hours of tedious work

> "Red Gate's SQL Data Generator has overnight become the principal tool we use for loading test data to run our performance and load tests"
> **Grant Fritchey** Principal DBA, FM Global

| TitleOfCourtesy | BirthDate | HireDate | Address | | | | |
Title	datetime	datetime	Address Line (5				
Dr	23/08/1963 04:0...	25/04/1992 20:0...	37 Fabien St.				
Miss	10/01/1960 23:2...	16/02/1976 11:2...	850 White Nobel...				
Mr	27/07/1970 13:5...	03/12/1953 15:3...	45 Green Milton...	New York	TN-OH	60387	Liberia
Mr	27/01/2002 04:3...	24/07/1958 00:5...	43 Milton Boulev...	Sacramento	NM-JR	13294	Côte d'Ivoir
Mr	31/05/1994 04:1...	12/01/1964 04:4...	592 Rocky Cowl...	Santa Ana	MI-UU	NULL	Jersey
Mrs	17/11/1975 10:1...	27/10/1968 18:5...	69 Clarendon Pa...	San Jose	IL-TC	41768	New Caledc
Dr.	16/05/1974 06:1...	25/11/1998 14:5...	207 Fabien Blvd.	Houston	AL-GE	04937	Belgium
Dr	27/12/1999 19:4...	03/05/1972 13:1...	53 Rocky Oak R...	Baton Rouge	MA-RT	65364	Swaziland
Dr	14/10/1971 03:1...	28/06/1978 10:0...	260 East Rocky...	Charlotte	AL-AR	97727	Benin
Mr	09/11/1981 13:2...	26/12/2001 15:0...	476 North Fabie...	Akron	MA-IU	94269	Palau
Dr	28/06/1987 01:3...	30/10/1972 00:0...	48 South Hague...	Norfolk	VT-UV	66385	American Si
Mr	20/10/1962 04:4...	07/09/2005 17:1...	939 Fabien Park...	Grand Rapids	HI-YT	86033	Swaziland
Mr	25/01/2001 08:0...	18/08/1983 12:0...	348 North Green...	Wichita	FL-IV	32302	Zambia

How to Become an Exceptional DBA

Brad McGehee

A career guide that will show you, step-by-step, exactly what you can do to differentiate yourself from the crowd so that you can be an Exceptional DBA. While Brad focuses on how to become an Exceptional SQL Server DBA, the advice in this book applies to any DBA, no matter what database software they use. If you are considering becoming a DBA, or are a DBA and want to be more than an average DBA, this is the book to get you started.

ISBN: 978-1-906434-05-2
Published: July 2008

SQL Server Execution Plans

Grant Fritchey

Execution plans show you what's going on behind the scenes in SQL Server and provide you with a wealth of information on how your queries are being executed. Grant provides a clear route through the subject, from the basics of capturing plans, through their interpretation, and then right on to how to use them to understand how you might optimize your SQL queries, improve your indexing strategy, and so on. All this rich information makes the execution plan a fairly important tool in the tool belt of pretty much anyone who writes TSQL to access data in a SQL Server database.

ISBN: 978-1-906434-02-1
Published: June 2008

The Best of SQL Server Central
Brad McGehee

Once again SQLServerCentral.com had another fantastic year and "Best of SQL Server Central - Vol 6" pulls together the best, the most popular, and the most read articles of 2008,
in handy dead tree format, covering database administration, BI, design, security, T-SQL, and most things in between.

ISBN: 978-1-906434-07-6
Published: June 2009

SQL Server Tacklebox
Rodney Landrum

As a DBA, how well-prepared are you to tackle 'monsters' such as backup failure due to lack of disk space, or locking and blocking that is preventing critical business processes from running, or data corruption due to a power failure in the disk subsystem? If you have any hesitation in your answers to these questions, then Rodney Landrum's SQL Server Tacklebox is a must-read.

ISBN: 978-1-906434-25-0
Published: August 2009